CONTENTS

Acknowledgements

The author and publishers wish to thank the following who have kindly given permission for the use of copyright material:

Anthony Burton and Murray Pollinger for extracts from *The Rainhill Story*, BBC Publications (1980); T. Coleman for extracts from *The Railway Navvies*, Hutchinson Publishing Group Ltd. (1965); Hunter Davies for extracts from *George Stephenson*, George Weidenfeld & Nicolson Ltd. (1975); Frank Ferneyhough for extracts from *Liverpool and Manchester Railway 1830–1980*, Robert Hale Ltd. (1980); J.R. Kellett for extracts from *The Impact of Railways on Victorian Cities*, Routledge & Kegan Paul PLC (1969); R.H.G. Thomas for extracts from *The Liverpool and Manchester Railway*, B.T. Batsford Ltd. (1980).

Every effort has been made to trace all the copyright holders, but if any have been inadvertently overlooked the publishers will be pleased to make the necessary arrangement at the first opportunity.

The author and publishers wish to acknowledge, with thanks, the following photographic sources:

BBC Hulton Picture Library, pp. 6 right, 12, 23, 42, 47 left; British Railways LM Region, Publicity Department, p. 20 right; Mary Evans Picture Library, p. 8; *Illustrated London News*, p. 43; The Mansell Collection, pp. 6 left, 7, 10, 11, 13, 20 left, 22, 28, 30, 32, 36 top, 37, 46, 50; by kind permission of the trustees of the Science Museum, London, pp. 15, 19, 21, 25, 26 top, 36 bottom, 41, 47 right, 48, 55.

PREFACE

The study of history is exciting, whether in a good story well told, a mystery solved by the judicious unravelling of clues, or a study of the men, women and children whose fears and ambitions, successes and tragedies make up the collective memory of mankind.

This series aims to reveal this excitement to pupils through a set of topic books on important historical subjects from the Middle Ages to the present day. Each book contains four main elements: a narrative and descriptive text, lively and relevant illustrations, extracts of contemporary evidence, and questions for further thought and work. Involvement in these elements should provide an adventure which will bring the past to life in the imagination of the pupil.

Each book is also designed to develop the knowledge, skills and concepts so essential to a pupil's growth. It provides a wide, varying introduction to the evidence available on each topic. In handling this evidence, pupils will increase their understanding of basic historical concepts such as causation and change, as well as of more advanced ideas such as revolution and democracy. In addition, their use of basic study skills will be complemented by more sophisticated historical skills such as the detection of bias and the formulation of opinion.

The intended audience for the series is pupils of eleven to sixteen years: it is expected that the earlier topics will be introduced in the first three years of secondary school, while the nineteenth and twentieth century topics are directed towards first examinations.

385

947.07

THE EARLY RAILWAYS 1825-50

S. M. Harrison

Head of Humanities, Knutsford County High School, Cheshire

M
MACMILLAN
EDUCATION

To Miles, Julian and Lisa

© S.M. Harrison 1986

All rights reserved. No reproduction, copy or transmission
of this publication may be made without written permission.

No paragraph of this publication may be reproduced, copied
or transmitted save with written permission or in accordance
with the provisions of the Copyright Act 1956 (as amended),
or under the terms of any licence permitting limited copying
issued by the Copyright Licensing Agency, 33−4 Alfred Place,
London WC1E DP.

Any person who does any unauthorised act in relation to
this publication may be liable to criminal prosecution and
civil claims for damages.

First published 1986
Reprinted 1987 (twice)

Published by
MACMILLAN EDUCATION LTD
Houndmills, Basingstoke, Hampshire RG21 2XS
and London
Companies and representatives
throughout the world

Printed in Hong Kong

British Library Cataloguing in Publication Data
Harrison, Scott Michael
The Early Railways. — (History in Depth)
1. Railroad — Great Britain — History — 19th century
I. Title   II. Series
385′.0941   HE3018
ISBN 0−333−38712−0

INTRODUCTION

A book published in 1849, only 24 years after the opening of the first public steam railway, was introduced with this story:

> *A good many years ago, one of the toughest and hardest riders that ever crossed Leicestershire undertook to perform a feat which, just for the moment, attracted the general attention not only of the country but of the sporting world. His bet was, that, if he might choose his own turf, and if he might select as many thorough-bred horses as he liked, he would undertake to ride 200 miles in ten hours!*
>
> *The newspapers of the day described exactly how 'the Squire' was dressed — what he had been living on — how he looked — how, at the word 'Away!' he started like an arrow from a bow — how gallantly Tranby, his favourite racer, stretched himself in his gallop — how, on arriving at his second horse, he vaulted from one saddle to another — how he then flew over the surface of the earth, if possible, faster than before — and how, to the astonishment and amidst the acclamations of thousands of spectators, he at last came in ... a winner!*
>
> *Now, if at this moment of his victory, while with dust and perspiration on his brow, a decrepit old woman had hobbled forward, and in the name of Science had told the assembled multitude, that, before she became a skeleton, she and her husband would undertake, instead of 200 miles in 10 hours, to go 500 — that is to say, that, for every mile 'the Squire' had just ridden, she and her old man would go two miles and a half — that she would moreover knit all the way, and that he should take his medicine every hour and read to her just as if they were at home; lastly, that they would undertake to perform their feat either in darkness or in daylight, in sunshine or in storm, 'in thunder, lightning, or in rain,' — who, we ask, would have listened to the poor maniac? — and yet how wonderfully would her prediction have been now fulfilled!*
>
> F.B. Head: *Stokers and Pokers*, 1849

acclamations: cheering

1

WANTED-A NEW TRANSPORT SYSTEM

Historians of the railways continue to argue about when and where railways were 'invented'. In this book the starting point will be 1818 in Darlington, and 1822 in Liverpool. There were railway lines in existence before these dates, and there were locomotives running on some of them, but there was no public railway. People did not know about railways, and nobody could foresee the great revolution in the transport system of this country.

In 1818 a committee met at Darlington to propose:

That a canal or Rail or Tram Road from the River Tees to the Collieries and the interior of the country will essentially promote as well the Agricultural as the Mining and Commercial interests of this District.

> Minutes of the meeting, quoted in
> Norman Moorsom's book,
> *The Stockton and Darlington Railway*, 1975

Seven years later their brainchild was born — a railway running from Stockton to Darlington. By that time a similar meeting had taken place in Liverpool. Subsequently, in 1830, the Liverpool and Manchester Railway was opened and people throughout the country began to realise that a new age of transport was upon them.

Two considerations must have been in the minds of those who attended the meetings in Darlington and Liverpool: the problems of the old system of transport, and the prospects for the new.

Catch me who can.

Above: *Trevithick's locomotive of 1804*

Right: *Hetton colliery – an early example of locomotives in use in industry*

The old system: roads and canals

The committee which met at Darlington came together to solve a particular problem: there were rich coalfields in the area, but by the time that the coal reached the markets, the cost of transportation had made it much dearer than rival Tyneside coal.

> *A single horsecart load of coal may, on average, be procured at the pit for four shillings. At Darlington this quantity sells for ten or twelve shillings, and at York and Stockton for sixteen or eighteen shillings.*
>
> Report Relative to a Communication from Stockton, by Darlington to the Collieries, 1818

The hazards of coaching

The problem in Lancashire was more general. Population, trade and industry were all growing fast, and the existing transport systems were unable to cope, although they had improved during the eighteenth century.

Francis, one of the first historians of the railways, looked back on recent developments in the transportation of passengers by road:

> *1712. Edenbro, Berwick, Newcastle, Durham and London Stage-coach, which performs the journey in thirteen days without stoppages (if God permits) having eighty able horses to perform the whole journey, each passenger paying four pounds ten shillings.*

> *1770. Notwithstanding the establishment of turnpikes in 1703, it is certain that by 1770 no great improvement had been effected ....
> Ruts four or five feet deep were common, even in summer, being primitively mended by rolling in large loose stones.*

> *1830. By the period of the railroad era it is fair to conclude that the coaching system was perfect. The cattle were changed in a few brief seconds; the coachmen were bound by heavy penalties to be at their destination at the appointed hour; horses were bred especially for the duty, and they were urged in some cases with such inexorable rigour that ... they fell with excitement and died of a broken blood vessel or a broken heart.*
>
> J. Francis: History of the English Railway, 1851

turnpikes: turnpike trusts were companies which undertook to maintain a stretch of road. In return for their services they charged a fee, which travellers paid at the turnpike gates

inexorable rigour: constant encouragement

The horses were not the only ones in danger. The railway pioneer George Stephenson (see page 11) was once travelling by coach when a wheel broke. The coach overturned but Stephenson was unhurt and was able to attend to the wounds of his fellow passengers. If, as Francis said, the road system was 'as perfect as could be', then the need for an alternative mode of transport was great indeed!

The committee at Darlington did give consideration to the idea of building canals, which were an existing alternative to the roads. However, the gradients in the area ruled out this suggestion, and the railway was chosen instead. In Lancashire they already had canals, but it was because they were as unsatisfactory as the roads that a railway was proposed:

The canal companies have enjoyed a virtual monopoly ... and they have abused their power and controlled their customers. The canal carriers have raised the freight of corn from 6s. 8d. to 12s. 6d. per ton, and that of cotton from 6s. 8d. to 15s. Although the facilities of transit were manifestly deficient, although the barges employed to carry the goods were sometimes wrecked by storms, although for ten days during the summer the canals were closed, although in winter they were frozen up for weeks ... yet they sent as much or as little as suited them, and shipped it how and when they pleased .... It sometimes occupied a longer time from Liverpool to Manchester than from Liverpool to New York.

Parliamentary papers

So much for the problems of road and canal — but what new opportunities might a new system of transport open up?

The canal at Littleborough

Great expectations: the prospects for railways

The committee at Darlington saw that a railway might benefit a great number of people:

The primary object is to supply with coal at a much cheaper rate than the present mode of conveyance a population of not less than 40,000 inhabitants .... [Coal] is now brought to them in carts on the turnpike road along which one horse scarcely drags one ton at the rate of 8d. or 9d. per ton per mile, whilst on the level line of railway one horse will take ten tons at the rate of about 3d. per ton per mile.

The lead mines will derive ... benefit, the agriculturalist also will carry his product to market and bring upon his farm a larger supply of lime and manure at much reduced expense. The railway will take off from the turnpikes all the heavy carriage which so materially injures them and occasions the present vast expense.

The population at large will benefit from the reduced price of fuel.

There is a reasonable prospect of your subscribers receiving 15% per annum.

Report to the Noblemen and Gentlemen,
Proprietors of Estates on the Adopted Line ... and to
an Enlightened and Liberal Public, February 1821

When the line was built, the committee was proved to be right, and it was not long before people from all walks of life saw some advantage in the coming of the railway. In 1834 a commission was set up by the House of Lords to hear evidence in support of a new line from London to Birmingham.

Amongst the people who spoke up in support of the line were merchants, an ironmonger, a silk manufacturer, a mason, a butcher, a dairy farmer, a secretary to a bank and a secretary to the Post Office. A grazier thought it would be better than walking his cattle to market:

Sometimes the poor things are driven till their feet are sore, and the effect of that is that they are sold on the road for what they can get. It is often the case that they drive many of them until they have not a foot to stand on.

A Quartermaster General in the army thought it would be better than walking his troops into action — sometimes!

In cases of emergency it would be very desirable to send troops by that mode of conveyance which would be very rapid and safe; in cases not of emergency, it is my opinion that troops should not be conveyed by either canal or carriage or railroad, but that they should be made to perform one of the most effective parts of military duty, to march.

Some, with a broader view, saw a fantastic future. They thought that the railways might

alter the whole system of our internal communication, substituting an agency whose ultimate effects can scarcely be anticipated.

Liverpool Mercury, 1825

Questions

1 What developments were affecting both the Stockton — Darlington and Liverpool — Manchester areas which made a better system of transport desirable?
2 When an early locomotive was brought from the north east of England to the north west, it was transported by sea as far as possible. What were the reasons for this?
3 Compare the description of passenger travel by road with a 'Christmas card' view of the age of coaching.
4 How much were the failings of the canal from Liverpool to Manchester due to the canal system itself, and how much due to management?
5 List the people who would gain from the railway according to the Stockton and Darlington publicity.
6 Select four of the people who were in favour of a line from London to Birmingham, and say what they might hope to gain from a new system of transport.

2

THE OPPOSITION TO RAILWAYS

The case against speed

Although the first railway lines were greeted with great excitement and enthusiasm by the general public, there was an influential group of people who stood firmly against the new invention for various reasons. At first they concentrated their attack on the danger of travelling at speed. Here are three contemporary opinions:

palpably: plainly

> *What can be more palpably absurd and ridiculous than the prospect held out of locomotives travelling twice as fast as stage-coaches.*

> *. . . monstrous, extraordinary, most dangerous and impracticable, and it would cause wholesale destruction of human life.*

> *. . . no locomotive could travel at 10 m.p.h., but if it does, I will undertake to eat a stewed engine wheel for breakfast.*

Once the locomotive had proved capable of ten miles an hour, the opposition moved on:

> *It is certainly some consolation to those who are to be whirled at the rate of eighteen or twenty miles an hour, by means of a high pressure engine, to be told that they are in no danger of being seasick while they are on shore, that they are not to be scalded to death or drowned by the bursting of the boiler, and that they need not mind being shot by the*

Beware the railway!

*scattered fragments or dashed in pieces by the flying off or the breaking
of a wheel.*

The Quarterly, 1825

A host of other complaints about the effects of locomotives were
related by the railway enthusiast and writer, Samuel Smiles:

*It was declared that [the railway] would prevent cows grazing and
hens laying. The poisoned air from the locomotive would kill birds as
they flew over them, and render the preservation of pheasants and
foxes no longer possible. Householders adjoining the projected line
were told that their houses would be burnt up by the fire thrown from
the engine chimneys; while the air around would be polluted by clouds
of smoke. There would no longer be any use for horses, and if the
railways were extended the species would become extinguished and
oats and hay rendered unsaleable.*

S. Smiles: *The Lives of George and Robert Stephenson, 1857*

*George Stephenson, the
founder of the English
railway system, was born
near Newcastle in 1781. He
did not go to school, but
learned about engines by
helping his father who
worked on the steam
engines at Wylam colliery*

Opposition in Parliament

The pamphlets, speeches, articles and cartoons against the railways
were intended to influence public opinion, but the real opposition
came when railway bills were put before Parliament. (Railways were
controversial and involved the compulsory purchase of land, so each
railway company needed the assent of Parliament.)

The case of the Liverpool and Manchester Railway is typical of the
problems of the early lines. Before putting their proposals to Parliament, the company had to draw up plans showing proposed routes,
time-scales and costs. George Stephenson, the chief engineer of the
Liverpool and Manchester Railway, wrote of problems facing his
surveyors:

*We have had sad work with Lord Derby, Lord Sefton and Brad-
shaw, the great Canal Proprietor, whose grounds we go through with
the projected railway. Their ground is blockaded on every side to
prevent us getting on with the Survey. Bradshaw fires guns through
his ground in the course of the night to prevent the surveyor roaming in
the dark. We are to have a grand field day next week. The Liverpool
Railway Company are determined to force a railway through if
possible. Lord Sefton says he will have a hundred men against us.*

Quoted in Hunter Davies' book, *George Stephenson, 1975*

Finally a survey of sorts was completed, and the battle moved to
Westminster. The debate in Parliament began in March 1825. Railways were little known in the south, and Stephenson was warned that
he should not lay too much stress on railway speed; if he claimed that
his locomotives could go at speeds of 20 miles per hour, 'he would be
regarded as a maniac fit for bedlam'. His lawyer therefore spoke only
of relatively low speeds.

bedlam: the nickname of the
hospital of St Mary of
Bethlehem in London, where
mad people were sent

The opposition lawyers questioned Stephenson on the subject of danger:

> *'Suppose, now, one of these engines to be going along the line at the rate of nine or ten miles per hour, and that a cow were to stray on the line and get in the way of the engine; would not that, think you, be a very awkward circumstance?'*

Stephenson replied:

> *'Yes, very awkward for the cow.'*

The lawyer continued:

> *'Would not animals be very much frightened by the engine passing them, especially by the glare of the red hot chimney?'*

Stephenson's unexpected reply was:

> *'But how would they know that it wasn't painted?'*

The fiercest opposition arose over the question of the building of the line. Here Stephenson was found to have made mistakes in his calculations, which gave opposition lawyers an opportunity to question his competence. Further, some parts of his plan were made to look ridiculous. In one place the proposed railway was to cross the River Irwell, a navigable waterway. Stephenson was questioned about his bridge:

> *'What is the width of the Irwell there?'*
> *'I cannot say exactly at present.'*
> *'How many arches is your bridge to have?'*
> *'It is not determined upon.'*
> *'How could you make an estimate for it then?'*
> *'I have given a sufficient sum for it.'*

Parliamentary papers

The Sankey Viaduct – a monument to Stephenson's eventual success

It is no wonder that, in his summing up, Mr Alderson (one of the opposition lawyers) was able to say:

> *Did any ignorance ever arrive at such a pitch as this? Was there ever any ignorance exhibited like this? Is Mr Stephenson to be the person upon whose faith this committee is to pass this bill involving property to the extent of £400,000 or £500,000, when he is so ignorant of his profession as to propose to build a bridge not sufficient to carry off the flood water of the river or to permit any of the vessels to pass, which of necessity must pass under it, and leave his own railroad liable to be several feet under water?*

Parliamentary papers

Another problem was Stephenson's plan to build the railway across the bog known as Chat Moss. A respected engineer, called before the Parliamentary committee, said:

> *No engineer in his senses would go through Chat Moss if he wanted to make a railroad from Liverpool to Manchester.*

Mr Alderson pursued the point:

> *Everyone knows Chat Moss — everyone knows that iron sinks immediately on its being put on the surface .... There is nothing, it appears, except long, sedgy grass and a little soil to prevent it sinking into the shades of eternal night. I have now done, sir, with Chat Moss, and there I leave this railroad.*

Parliamentary papers

Chat Moss – 'No engineer in his senses would go through Chat Moss'

Indeed, the railway was sunk. The bill was rejected and Stephenson was sacked. Worse still, a young engineer, Hugh Steele, who had made some of the errors in Stephenson's report, felt so badly about it that he committed suicide in Stephenson's Newcastle office.

Victory at last

The battle was lost, but not the war. The railway company commissioned a new survey, changed the most controversial parts of the route, and returned to Parliament with a new bill.

The opposition were becoming increasingly desperate, as shown by the frailty of the arguments put forward by Sir Isaac Coffin:

> *What was to be done with all those who advanced money in making and repairing turnpike roads? What was to become of coach makers and harness makers, coachmasters and coachmen, innkeepers, horse breeders and horse dealers?*
>
> Parliamentary papers

On this sort of argument, and with the strength of the railway promoters, the opposition was bound to fail. Even Lord Derby, one of the only two lords to oppose the bill, was later to write:

to accrue: to be gained

> *Although at the commencement of this fine work I thought myself fully justified in opposing it, I am now so well satisfied of the public benefit likely to accrue from its progress as sincerely to congratulate the committee on the accomplishment of their object.*
>
> Quoted in R.H.G. Thomas's book, *The Liverpool and Manchester Railway*, 1980

The victory for the Liverpool and Manchester Bill in 1826 did not, however, guarantee easy passage for the rest. Successive bills were contested tooth and nail, and it was not until the railway network was almost complete, 20 years later, that the opposition finally admitted defeat.

Questions

1 What interest groups appear to have been behind the opposition to the Liverpool and Manchester Railway? Give detailed reasons to support your answer.
2 Why do you think the opposition concentrated its main attack on the alleged danger of railways?
3 In the light of your answer to question 2, do you think that there were people who were genuinely afraid of railways?
4 Why did the first Liverpool and Manchester Railway Bill fail? In your answer you should consider: the nature of Parliament; the strength of the opposition; the uncertain future of railways; the survey; Stephenson.
5 Construct an effective piece of anti-railway propaganda — for example, a poster, a speech, a poem or a cartoon.

3

BUILDING THE LINES

Contractors and navvies

In the 20 years following the granting of permission to build the Liverpool and Manchester Railway, most of the lines in existence today were laid down. This was truly the railway revolution. Main lines linked the capital with the provinces, and these in turn were connected by a network which criss-crossed the country.

The actual laying down of the lines was a superhuman feat overseen by far-sighted engineers, managed by contractors with tight deadlines to meet, and made possible by the muscle power of the railway navvies who dug, blasted, mined and carted millions of tons of rock and earth. Each line has its own stories — of great endeavour, of tragedy, of setbacks and, in most cases, of eventual success.

The task of building a line of say, 80 kilometres, was formidable. Although some engineers maintained close overall control, it was normally the practice to segment the work and divide the responsibility. The diagram on page 16 shows the chain of command between the engineers and the navvies.

navvies: originally labourers who cut the canals, but the name stuck; other names such as 'bankers' were also used

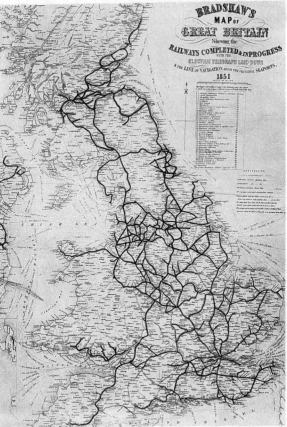

Bradshaw's map, 1839

Bradshaw's map, 1851

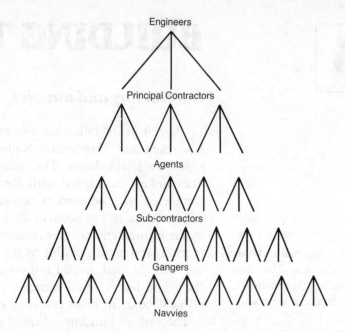

```
                    Engineers
                       /|\
                      / | \
                     /  |  \
              Principal Contractors
               /|\   /|\   /|\
                    Agents
            /|\ /|\ /|\ /|\ /|\
                 Sub-contractors
         /|\ /|\ /|\ /|\ /|\ /|\ /|\
                   Gangers
        /|\ /|\ /|\ /|\ /|\ /|\ /|\ /|\
                    Navvies
```

Thomas Brassey: one of the most famous contractors, he worked on the Great Western Railway before moving on to such places as the Crimea and Canada

Some of the contractors, such as Samuel Morton Peto or Thomas Brassey, built up their own armies of agents, sub-contractors and navvies. Sometimes they controlled the sub-contractors very closely. At other times the sub-contractors, having made a tender to complete a piece of work, were left alone. This could bring them great wealth, or ruin. A sub-contractor had to weigh up in his mind what a job would cost. His profit would be the difference between that figure and the amount he had to spend on materials and labour. Thus the tender was important:

> *One Mr Wythes [probably George Wythes, who undertook among other lines, that from Dorchester to Maiden Newton] ... was thinking of submitting an offer for a contract. He first thought £18,000 would be reasonable, but then consulted his wife and agreed it should be £20,000. Thinking it over he decided not to take any risk so made it £40,000. They slept on it and the next morning his wife said she thought he had better make it £80,000. He did; it turned out to be the lowest tender, and he founded his fortune on it.*
>
> T. Coleman: The Railway Navvies, 1965

Not all were so lucky. On the London — Birmingham line, of 30 contractors who gained a part of the work, ten failed. Some of the projects which ruined them will be described later in this chapter. Sub-contractors, having less capital, were even more likely to fail. The whole business was very hazardous; much depended on the relationship between the sub-contractor and his workmen, the infamous navvies.

Navvies had a fearful reputation. One of them, named Hobday, who had just been sentenced to 15 years' transportation for maiming a fellow navvy, was described as follows:

The prisoner Hobday is a remarkable man, and may be considered a type of the class to which he belongs. His stature is rather below the common height, but his broad frame gives evidence of immense strength. His countenance is forbidding in the extreme. Every feature indicates habitual crime —
'For evil passions cherished long,
Have ploughed them with expressions strong'
— while his matted hair completes the aspect of the finished ruffian. We understand he has said that for nine years he has never slept in a bed or worn a hat; that his custom was to put on his boots when new, and never remove them until they fell to pieces; and his clothes were treated very much in the same way, except that his shirt was changed once a week.

Carlisle Patriot, 1846

Rioting, drunkenness, gluttony and sinful living also formed part of the popular view.

The other side of the story shows the navvies as victims of terrible working and living conditions. The following table shows a typical list of injuries:

A LIST of RAILWAY ACCIDENTS admitted into the *Salisbury* Infirmary, from 23rd June 1845 to 30 May 1846.

Date of Admission.		No.	CASE.	When and how Discharged.	In the House.	
					Weeks.	Days.
23 June	1845 –	1	compound fracture – – –	died, 24 June 1845 –	–	1
14 August	– –	2	injury to the chest – – –	cured, 27 Sept.	6	2
1 Sept.	– –	3	wound of the arm – – – –	ditto, 13 Sept. – –	1	6
28 Sept.	– –	4	injury to the knee – – – –	ditto, 28 Oct.	4	2
21 August	– –	5	wound of the toe – – – –	ditto, 13 Sept.	3	2
13 August	– –	6	wound of the scalp – – –	ditto, 30 August	2	4
13 August	– –	7	contusions – – – – – – –	ditto, 13 Sept.	4	3
12 Sept.	– –	8	fractured pelvis – – – – –	died, 12 Sept.	–	1
11 October	– –	9	lacerated face – – – – –	cured, 1 Nov.	3	–
28 October	– –	10	wound of the scalp – – –	ditto, 15 Nov.	2	4
30 October	– –	11	wound of the scalp – – –	ditto, 22 Nov.	3	2
8 October	– –	12	amputated toe – – – – –	ditto, 29 Nov.	7	3
27 Sept.	– –	13	fractured humerus – – –	ditto, 29 Nov.	9	–
4 Nov.	– –	14	concussion of the brain – –	ditto, 6 Dec.	4	4
24 Nov.	– –	15	contusions – – – – –	ditto, 16 Dec.	3	–
12 Sept.	– –	16	fractured thigh — – – – –	ditto, 16 Dec.	13	3
12 Dec.	– –	17	contusions – – – – – – –	ditto, 20 Dec.	1	1
12 Sept.	– –	18	injury to the spine – – – –	ditto, 20 Dec.	14	1
27 October	– –	19	crushed hand, amputated –	ditto, 10 Jan. 1846 –	10	5
16 January	1846 –	20	fractured ribs – – – – – –	ditto, 20 Feb.	5	–
28 October	1845 –	21	injury to the knee – – – –	ditto, 31 Jan. – –	13	4
31 Dec.	– –	22	injury to the back – – – –	ditto, 8 Feb. – –	5	4
27 Jan.	– –	23	lacerated hand – – – – –	ditto, 14 Feb.	2	4
31 Jan.	– –	24	injury to the testicle – – –	ditto, 14 Feb.	2	–
3 Jan.	– –	25	bruised foot – – – – –	ditto, 14 Feb.	6	–
16 Jan.	– –	26	sprained ankle – – – – –	ditto, 28 Feb.	6	1
20 Feb.	– –	27	lacerated face – – – – –	ditto, 7 March	2	1
21 Feb.	1846 –	28	acute rheumatism – – – –	ditto, 14 March	3	–
16 March	– –	29	contusions – – – – – – –	ditto, 21 March	–	5
28 Feb.	– –	30	wound of the elbow – – –	ditto, 28 March	4	–
13 March	– –	31	contusions – – – – – –	ditto, 28 March	2	1
4 Feb.	– –	32	– compound fracture, amputation.	ditto, 2 May	12	3
27 Jan.	– –	33	compound fracture – – –	ditto, 9 May	14	4
6 May	– –	34	contusions – – – – – – –	ditto, 9 May	–	3
12 March	– –	35	fractured thigh – – – – –	ditto, 23 May	10	2
14 April	– –	36	wound of the foot – – – –	ditto, 23 May	5	4
9 Jan.	– –	37	wound of the scalp – – –	ditto, 27 Jan.	2	4
13 Feb.	– –	38	wound of the hand – – –	ditto, 26 Feb.	1	6
17 Feb.	– –	39	injury of the wrist – – – –	ditto, 8 March	2	5
8 Jan.	– –	40	contusions – – – – – – –	ditto, 18 Jan.	1	3
18 March	– –	41	contusions – – – – – – –	ditto, 27 March	1	2
7 March	– –	42	sprained foot – – – – –	ditto, 15 April	5	4
20 May	– –	43	abscess in the axilla – – –	still in the house	1	3
7 May	– –	44	crushed leg, amputated – –	– – ditto –	3	2
30 March	– –	45	crushed thigh – – – – –	– – ditto –	8	5
15 April	– –	46	fractured leg – – – – – –	– – ditto –	6	3
20 May	– –	47	rheumatic fever – – – – –	– – ditto –	1	3
8 Jan.	– –	48	compound fracture – – –	– – ditto –	20	2
12 Jan.	– –	49	compound fracture – – –	– – ditto –	19	5
20 March	– –	50	lacerated wound of the thigh	– – ditto –	10	1
12 March	– –	51	fractured thigh – – – – –	– – ditto –	11	2
14 April	– –	52	crushed foot, amputated –	– – ditto –	6	4

In addition to the above list, a large number of railway labourers have been relieved at the Infirmary as casual or out-patients.

The navvies shared the risk of a sub-contractor going broke and being unable to pay wages. Although they were often paid well, they could easily be exploited by unscrupulous contractors operating the 'truck' system:

> *A man comes and applies for work and the contractor asks him if he has any money; he says he has none and the contractor says 'Then you must have food, and I will give you a line to such a house where you will be supplied with what you require until your wages come due'. The wages are not payable generally for a month after the engagement ... and at the end of the period whatever he has expended is deducted from the amount of the wage he receives. [The contractor] guarantees the person who furnishes the food his payment out of the wages of the labourers, and for that he receives five per cent; I have heard it stated at more.*
>
> Select Committee on Railway Labourers, 1846

The truck system was at its worst when the workers were paid in tokens so that they could only buy from the truck shop. Goods available from these shops were often substandard and overpriced. No wonder there was trouble. Yet Samuel Morton Peto, who knew the navvies well, wrote:

> *I knew from personal experience that if you pay him well and show you care for him, he is the most faithful creature in existence; but if you find him working for fourpence a day, and that paid in potatoes and meal, can we wonder that the results are as we find them.*
>
> T. Coleman: *The Railway Navvies*, 1965

Questions

1 Look at the maps on page 15, then describe:
   a) the extent of the railway system by 1839
   b) how the system had grown between 1839 and 1851.
2 Look at the diagram showing the organisation of work, and accompanying description on page 16. What advantages did this system have for
   a) the company
   b) the contractors and sub-contractors
   c) the navvies?
3 Look at the article from the *Carlisle Patriot* on page 17.
   How much *fact* is there in this article?
   How well substantiated are the opinions given here?
   Why might the readers of this paper have believed the article unquestioningly, in spite of the answers you have given above?
4 What are the dangers for the labourer in the 'truck' system, as outlined above?

The workings

gangers: senior navvies who took on, organised and even paid the labourers

Having had a tender accepted, the sub-contractor with his gangers and teams of navvies set about building a section of line.

The main problem was to keep to a level. Gradients were avoided wherever possible by building embankments, making cuttings, digging tunnels and erecting bridges. Most lines have amazing stories of how the teams overcame the physical problems which faced them. Here are a few examples of those which faced the men working for George Stephenson and his son Robert.

Robert Stephenson: born near Newcastle in 1803, he was given a good education in engineering before teaming up with his father, George, and becoming famous in his own right

Constructing an embankment

Chat Moss, described by Samuel Smiles as 'an immense bog of about twelve square miles, a mass of spongy vegetable pulp, the result of the growth and decay of ages, one year's growth rising upon another':

> *At some points embankment after embankment disappeared gradually and silently into the moss. [Stephenson's] men shod themselves with planks like skis, to sustain their weight by spreading its pressure.*
>
> T. Coleman: *The Railway Navvies*, 1965

theodolyte: instrument used by surveyors

> *The moss was very wet at the time ... and one day, when endeavouring to obtain a stand for his theodolyte, [Mr James] felt himself suddenly sinking. He immediately threw himself down and rolled over and over until he reached the ground again.*
>
> *Yet at last Stephenson conquered the moss. On overlapping hurdles made of branches and of the heather and brushwood that grew there, he laid sand, earth and gravel, thickly coated with cinders, until at last he got a firm but elastic road to carry the railway.*
>
> Quoted in F. Ferneyhough's book, *Liverpool and Manchester Railway 1830–1980*, 1980

Wolverton Embankment, 2.5 kilometres long, London and Birmingham Railway:

The Wolverton Embankment

> *... a loaded truck was detached from the train and a horse hitched*

to it ... not directly in front, but to the side of the track. The horse was made to walk, then trot, then gallop. When the truck got near the embankment edge the man running with the horse detached its halter, gave it a signal it had been taught to obey, and horse and man leaped aside. But the truck continued until it struck a bank of wood laid across the end of the track, when it tipped forwards, ejecting its contents over the edge of the bank.

T. Coleman: *The Railway Navvies*, 1965

Making a cutting

Olive Mount Cutting, Liverpool and Manchester Railway:

It ran for nearly two miles and at its deepest was over a hundred feet. Using a large team, nearly half a million tons, much of it solid rock, was dug or blasted out. It looked as if it had been dug out by giants.

S. Smiles: *The Lives of George and Robert Stephenson*, 1857

Blisworth Cutting, London and Birmingham Railway:

The cutting ... is 1½ miles long, and in some places 54 feet deep, passing through earth, stiff clay, and hard rock. A million cubic yards of these materials were dug, quarried and blasted out of it ....
Beneath the stone lay a thick bed of clay, under which were found beds of loose shale so full of water that constant pumping was

Right: *Olive Mount*

Below: *Making a cutting*

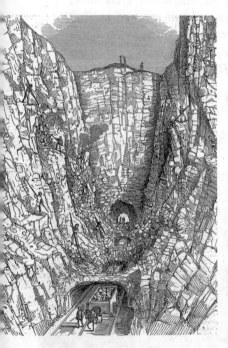

20

Tring Cutting

necessary. *Steam engines were set to pump out the water, locomotives to drag away the excavated rock and clay; and 800 men and boys were employed in digging, wheeling and blasting, besides a large number of horses. Twenty-five barrels of gunpowder were used weekly; the total quantity exploded in forming this one cutting being about 3,000 barrels.*

S. Smiles: *The Lives of George and Robert Stephenson*, 1857

Men had taken to riding on a temporary tramway which was designed to take soil from a cutting to an embankment. One man was killed when a truck was derailed ... a few days later a gang of navvies riding down to their dinner were thrown off and buried beneath the derailed trucks.

F.B. Head: *Stokers and Pokers*, 1849

Tring Cutting, London and Birmingham Railway:

'Making the running' was the most spectacular part of navvy work and one of the most dangerous. The runs were made by laying planks up the side of the cutting, up which barrows were wheeled. The running was performed by the strongest of men. A rope, attached to the barrow and also to each man's belt, ran up the side of the cutting and then round a pulley at the top. When the barrow was loaded, a signal was given to the horse drawer at the top, and the man was drawn up the side of the cutting, balancing the barrow in front of him ... if on the upward climb the horse slipped or faltered, or if the man lost his balance on the muddy plank, then he had to do his best to save himself by throwing the loaded barrow to one side of the plank, and himself to the other.

At Tring there were 30–40 horse runs, and nearly all the navvies were thrown down the slope several times, but they got so used to it, and became so sure-footed, that only one man was killed.

T. Coleman: *The Railway Navvies*, 1965

Newcastle High Bridge

Bridges

The Sankey Viaduct, Liverpool and Manchester Railway:

> *The principal piece of masonry was the Sankey Viaduct. This fine work is principally of bricks with stone facings. It consists of nine arches of fifty feet span each. The massive piers are supported on two hundred piles driven deeply into the soil; and they rise to a great height, the coping of the parapet being seventy feet above the level of the valley.*
>
> S. Smiles: *The Lives of George and Robert Stephenson*, 1857

The High Level Bridge, Newcastle and Berwick Railway:

> *... by far the grandest work of the kind ... was the High Level Bridge ....*
>
> *The problem was, to throw a railway bridge across the deep ravine which lies between the towns of Newcastle and Gateshead .... The breadth of the river at the point of crossing is 515 feet, but the length of the bridge and viaduct between the Gateshead station and the terminus on the Newcastle side is about 4,000 feet ....*
>
> *The first difficulty ... was in securing a solid foundation for the piers. The dimensions of the piles to be driven were so huge that the engineer found it necessary to employ ... Nasmyth's titanic steam hammer.*
>
> *When the piles had been driven and the coffer dams formed, the water within the enclosed spaces was pumped out ... to lay bare the bed of the river. Considerable difficulty was experienced in the middle pier, in consequence of the water forcing itself through the quicksand beneath as fast as it was removed. This fruitless labour went on for months ... [until] cement concrete was at last put within the coffer dam until it set. A bed of concrete was laid up to the level of the heads of the piles ... and building proceeded ... 400,000 cubic feet of ashlar rubble and concrete were worked up in the piers.*
>
> *The most novel feature of the structure is the use of cast and wrought iron in forming the double bridge.*
>
> *The result is a bridge that for massive solidity may be pronounced unrivalled. It is perhaps the most magnificent and striking of all the bridges to which railways have given birth, and has been worthily styled 'The King of Railway Structures'.*
>
> S. Smiles: *The Lives of George and Robert Stephenson*, 1857

Tunnels

Wapping Tunnel, Liverpool and Manchester Railway:

> *Night and day the excavation proceeded .... In some places the substance excavated was a soft blue shale, with abundance of water;*

superincumbent mass: the material overhead

in other places a wet sand presented itself, requiring no slight labour to support, until the masonry which was to form the roof was erected. In passing under Crow Street, for want of sufficient props, the superincumbent mass fell in from the surface, being a depth of 30 feet of loose moss, earth and sand. On some occasions the miners refused to work, and it not infrequently required the personal superintendence and encouragement of the engineer to keep them at their posts. Nor is this surprising considering the nature of the operation. Boring their way almost in the dark with water streaming around them, and uncertain whether the props and stays would bear the pressure from above till the archwork should be completed ... the light of a few candles barely sufficient to show the dreariness of the place.

H. Booth: *The Liverpool and Manchester Railway,* 1830

Kilsby Tunnel, London and Birmingham Railway:

In order to drive the tunnel it was deemed necessary to construct 18 working shafts .... All of a sudden it was ascertained, that at about 200 yards from the south end of the tunnel there existed a hidden quicksand ... which the trial shafts had just passed without touching ... the quicksand in question covered several square miles.

The tunnel, 30 feet high by 30 feet broad, arched at the top as well as the bottom, was formed of bricks laid in cement, and the bricklayers were progressing in lengths averaging 12 feet when those who were nearest the quicksand, or driving into the roof, were suddenly almost overwhelmed by a deluge of water which burst in upon them. As it was evident that no time was to be lost, a gang of workmen, protected by the extreme power of the engines, were with their materials placed on a raft.

23

In spite of every effort to keep it down, the water rose with such rapidity that the men were near being jammed against the roof. The assistant engineer jumped overboard. Then, swimming with the rope in his mouth, he towed the raft to the foot of the nearest working shaft through which he and his men were safely lifted up into daylight.

By the strength of 1,250 men, 200 horses and 13 steam engines, not only was the work gradually completed, but during night and day, for eight months, the astonishing and almost incredible quantity of 1,800 gallons per minute from the quicksand alone was raised by Mr R. Stephenson and conducted away.

Indeed, such is the eagerness with which workmen in such cases proceed that, on a comrade being one day killed at their site by falling down the shaft, they merely, like sailors in action, chucked his body out of the way and then instantly proceeded with their work. In the construction of the tunnel there were lost 26 men.

F.B. Head: *Stokers and Pokers*, 1849

Questions

1 In your exercise book copy the cross-section of the Liverpool and Manchester Railway. Label the key points and briefly describe the problems faced at each of them.

The Liverpool – Manchester Railway

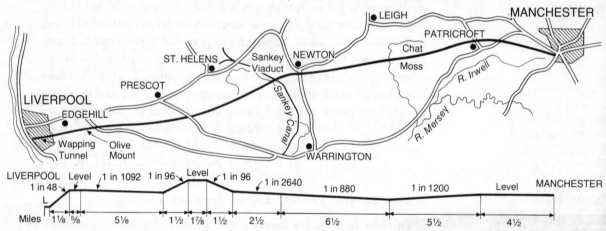

2 Use the illustrations and descriptions in this chapter to draw and label diagrams showing the processes involved in making embankments and cuttings.

3 On page 16 tendering for contracts was mentioned. Using the evidence given in this chapter, say why tendering was such a chancy business.

4 Look back at the table of accidents on page 17. Using the table and the evidence, list the most common injuries, then describe the sort of accidents that might have caused them.

5 What problems were created for the railway builders by water, and how were these problems overcome?

4

POWER AND SPEED

Early engines

When, in 1818, the Stockton and Darlington line was first proposed, few people knew about steam power and it was assumed by many that wagons would be towed along the lines by horses. However, there were already places where steam was being harnessed for transport. One system was to use stationary engines which wound in a length of rope, pulling wagons along a line. A series of stationary engines could, in theory, be used to power a whole railway.

Another system using steam was the locomotive. In 1804 a Cornishman, Richard Trevithick, had first displayed a travelling engine at work in order to win a bet. By 1818 other locomotives had been developed. Some of these were peculiar and highly dangerous — for example, William Brunton's experimental locomotive was propelled by two iron legs which walked along the track. This engine exploded in 1815, killing several people.

In spite of the fact that some locomotives were put to work in the collieries of the north east, they were so temperamental that few people saw any future in them. In a nutshell:

The basic problem was lack of steam power, the jerky motion caused by the roughly made gear wheels, which made most engines fall to pieces; the difficulty of regulating the valves and gears to put the engine in reverse; the overall heaviness of the machine, its slowness, and the brittle condition of the rails.

Hunter Davies: *George Stephenson*, 1975

George Stephenson was one of the pioneers who sought to overcome these problems. He was a self-taught engineer who built his first locomotive, *Blücher*, in 1814. He soon improved the engine with suitable modifications, and developed new rails which could bear the heavy load. The outcome was a working railway at his home in Killingworth, County Durham; by 1819 the line was 13 kilometres long and used both locomotives and stationary engines.

These developments were little known and the struggle to produce a viable locomotive occupied only a few inventive minds. However, when Stephenson was appointed as engineer to the Stockton and Darlington Railway, he brought with him the conviction that the line should carry locomotives. Here is a newspaper account of the opening of that railway:

So early as half past five o'clock in the morning a number of waggons, fitted up with seats, were fully occupied and they proceeded [drawn by horses] along the railway from Darlington towards the permanent steam engine.

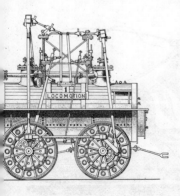

Locomotion, *an early success for Stephenson*

The opening of the
Stockton–Darlington
Railway

aspirations: puffs

*At about eight o'clock 13 waggons, 12 of them laden with two tons
of coal each, and the other with sacks of flour, the whole covered with
people, were drawn up the inclined plane of Brussleton in admirable
style. This inclined plane is . . . above a mile and a half long, yet
by means of two powerful steam engines erected at the top . . . the
waggons with their immense load were drawn up in eight minutes.*

*The waggons descended on the other side of the hill . . . and took
their station on the level below. . . . The hour of ten arrived before
all was ready to start. About this time the locomotive engine, or 'steam
horse', as it was more generally termed, gave 'note of preparation' by
some heavy aspirations, which seemed to excite astonishment and
alarm among the 'Johnny Raws' who had been led by curiosity to
the spot, and who, when a portion of steam was let off, fled in affright
. . . under the idea, we suppose, that some horrible explosion was
about to take place.*

*The scene, on the moving of the engine, sets description at defiance
. . . . Astonishment was not confined to the human species, for the
beasts of the field and the fowls of the air seemed to view with wonder
and awe the machine, which now moved onward at a rate of 10 or 12
m.p.h. with a weight of not less than 80 tons attached to it.*

*. . . The distance from Brussleton to Stockton is twenty and a half
miles, and the entire length . . . from Witton Park Colliery, nearly 25
miles, being, we believe, the largest railway in the Kingdom. The
whole population of the towns and villages within a few miles of the
Railway seem to have turned out, and we believe we speak within the
limits of truth, when we say that not less than 40 or 50,000 persons
were assembled to witness the proceedings of the day.*

Durham County Advertiser, 1 October 1825

A horse–powered railway

1 Read the newspaper report, then draw a simple diagram showing the different types of power used on the Stockton and Darlington line, in the order that the passengers would have experienced them.
2 In what ways does the newspaper report convey the atmosphere of amazement at this new development?
3 Is there anything in the report to indicate that, in spite of the astonishing events of the day, the reporter has tried not to exaggerate his account?

The Rainhill Trials

Locomotion, the railway engine on the Stockton and Darlington line, performed well and won some people over to the idea of locomotives. Even so, the directors of the Liverpool and Manchester line were far from convinced. They were bombarded with suggestions for new systems of railway power, as Samuel Smiles related:

Atmospheric pressure: atmospheric engines were designed to move trains by air pressure or vacuum along a continuous tube containing a piston attached to the train

> *There were plans for working the waggons along the line by water power. Some proposed hydrogen and others carbonic acid gas. Atmospheric pressure had its eager advocates, and various kinds of fixed and locomotive steam power were suggested.*

In this climate it is no wonder that the supporters of steam locomotives did not want to appear too ambitious. One such supporter wrote:

promulgate: spread

> *It is far from my wish to promulgate to the world that the ridiculous expectations ... of the enthusiastic specialist will be realised and that we shall see them travelling at the rate of 12, 16, 18, or 20 miles an hour; nothing could do more harm towards their adoption than the promulgation of such nonsense.*
>
> N. Wood: *A Practical Treatise on Railroads*, 1825

To resolve the problem, the Liverpool and Manchester committee decided to run a competition.

To Engineers and Iron Founders

The Directors of the Liverpool and Manchester Railway hereby offer a premium of £500 (over above the cost price) for a LOCOMOTIVE ENGINE which shall be a decided improvement on any hitherto constructed.

Weight limit 6 tons, 6 wheels
4 tons, 4 wheels.

A 6-ton engine must be capable of drawing after it, day by day, on a well-constructed railway, on a level plane, a train of carriages of the gross weight of twenty tons ... at the rate of Ten Miles per hour, with a pressure of steam on the boiler not exceeding fifty pounds on the square inch.

It is difficult for us to imagine quite what these engineers were being asked to do. The decision to have a competition was made on 20 April 1829. The trial to find a winner was to be held on 6 October 1829. In under six months competitors had to design, build, test and transport their engines. Admittedly some were in a position of advantage. As we have seen, the Stephensons had experience of building and running locomotives in the north east. So too did Timothy Hackworth, whose *Royal George* was the most successful locomotive on the Stockton and Darlington line. However, neither Stephenson's *Locomotion* nor Hackworth's *Royal George* would do for this competition — the one being unreliable, the other too cumbersome. Both men had to go back to the drawing board.

Two other competitors, John Braithwaite and John Ericsson, had no experience of locomotives at all. They were inventors, willing to turn their hands to any new challenge. They managed to design and build an engine for this competition in only seven weeks.

Finally the engineers assembled at Rainhill, which had been chosen for the trials because of its flatness.

On the morning of the 6th the ground at Rainhill presented a lively appearance, and there was as much excitement as if the St. Leger were about to be run. Many thousand spectators looked on, amongst whom were some of the first engineers and mechanicians of the day. A stand was provided for the ladies; the 'beauty and fashion' of the neighbourhood were present, and the side of the railroad was lined with carriages of all descriptions.

The Rainhill Trials

S. Smiles: *The Lives of George and Robert Stephenson*, 1857

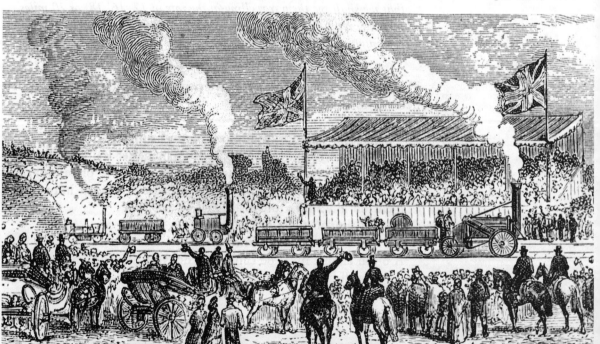

Name of locomotive and competitor	Origin	Appearance	Performance 1st day	2nd day	3rd day	4th day	5th day	6th day
Novelty J. Braithwaite & J. Ericsson	London — brought to Rainhill by canal	Light copper and blue; nippy	Reached 28 m.p.h. with no load	Broke bellows at 20 m.p.h.	Under repair	Reached 30 m.p.h. with 45 passengers	Under repair	Boiler gave way
Sans Pareil T. Hackworth	Darlington — brought by road	Green, yellow and black; overweight — broke the rules	Reached 18 m.p.h with no load	Exhibition run only; boiler defect	Under repair	Under repair	Made seven runs up to 14 m.p.h. but with heavy deposit of cinders; feed pump failed and burned out	
Rocket G. Stephenson	Newcastle — brought by road and steamship, then assembled and painted	Yellow, black, white chimney	Hauled 12½ tons at 12 m.p.h. Reached 25 m.p.h. without load. Little smoke but some cinders	Several successful runs	Twenty runs at up to 30 m.p.h.	Demon- stration runs up to 30 m.p.h. unladen		
Cycloped Brandreth	Liverpool	Powered by a horse walking on a drive belt	Went up to 5 m.p.h.	Some exhibition runs	Disqualified			
Perseverance Burstall	Edinburgh — damaged *en route* when wagon overturned	Red wheels	Under repair	Under repair	Under repair	Under repair	Under repair	Reached 6 m.p.h. then withdrew

The performance of the *Rocket* in the Rainhill Trials was overwhelming and George Stephenson and his partner, Henry Booth, took the prize as well as the contract to provide locomotives for the Liverpool and Manchester Railway. However, not everyone was satisfied with the result.

> *Timothy Hackworth has been sadly out of temper ever since he came for he has been grobbing on day and night ... he openly accused G.S.'s people of conspiring to hinder him.*
>
> Quoted in Hunter Davies' book, *George Stephenson*, 1975

> *Hackworth and his team made no secret of their dissatisfaction. Some of his supporters sourly hinted that as both the railway company's principal engineer and its treasurer were involved with the* Rocket, *only one result could be expected.*
>
> Hunter Davies: *George Stephenson*, 1975

Using the evidence: did the Rocket *win a fair victory?*
Consider the following evidence to see whether Hackworth's suspicions were justified:

A *The* Rocket *was entered by George and Robert Stephenson, and Henry Booth, who was Secretary and Treasurer of the Liverpool and Manchester Railway.*

Science Museum leaflet

B *Three eminent engineers were appointed as judges — John Raistrick, Nicholas Wood and John Kennedy. To the chagrin of*

stationary engines: even
after locomotives had
proved their worth,
stationary engines were
used on steep gradients to
haul trains by cable

his old friend George Stephenson, Raistrick tended to favour stationary engines. Wood, some years younger than Stephenson, had worked with the master from Blücher days, knew Robert as a boy, and believed in the steam locomotive. . . . John Kennedy, a Quaker of Manchester, had made his fortune by inventing textile machinery. A supporter of the locomotive, he had joined the railway promoters in 1822.

F. Ferneyhough: *Liverpool and Manchester Railway 1830–1980*, 1980

C *Hackworth faced enormous problems. . . . He had no factory of his own. . . . The manufacture of his parts had to be entrusted to local firms. Longridge manufactured the boiler. Stephenson's cast the cylinder, and other firms built other components.*

A Burton: *The Rainhill Story*, 1980

D Hackworth's own words:

Suffice it to say that neither in construction nor in principle was the engine deficient . . . but circumstances . . . compelled me to put that confidence in others which I found with sorrow was but too implicitly placed, as the defect [was] a cylinder which failed from its defective casting.

Quoted in A. Burton's book, *The Rainhill Story*, 1980

E *The* Sans Pareil *was not ready until the 13th; and when its boiler and tender were filled with water, it was found to weigh 4 cwt beyond the weight specified in the published conditions as the limit of four wheeled engines, nevertheless the judges allowed it to run on the same footing as other engines.*

S. Smiles: *The Lives of George and Robert Stephenson*, 1857

F *There were no design features which could not be found in existing engines so there was no sense in which it could have been said to point the path forward.* Sans Pareil *was a dead end . . . in some respects the design was retrogressive.*

A. Burton: *The Rainhill Story*, 1980

G *The* Rocket *of Mr Robert Stephenson . . . is a large and strongly built engine and went with a velocity which as long as the spectators had nothing to compare it with, they thought surprising enough. . . . The faults most perceptible in this engine were a great inequality in its velocity, and a very partial fulfillment of the condition that it should effectually consume its own smoke.*

The Novelty *and train*

The next engine . . . was the Novelty. *The great lightness of this engine (it is about one half lighter than Mr Stephenson's), its compactness and its beautiful workmanship excited universal admiration; a sentiment speedily changed into perfect wonder by its truly marvellous performances.*

Mechanics Magazine, 1829

1 Read sources **A** and **B**. Would you agree with the suggestion that Stephenson's contacts made victory for the *Rocket* more probable? Explain your answer.
2 Read sources **C** and **D**. Explain the difficulties which faced Hackworth in the manufacture of his locomotive. What does he refer to with 'sorrow'?
3 Read sources **E** and **F**. What light do these extracts throw on the attitude of the judges and the prospects of *Sans Pareil*?
4 Read source **G**. Was the *Rocket* the popular favourite?
5 Study the performance chart. How conclusive was the victory of the *Rocket*?
6 Summarise your opinion: did the *Rocket* win fairly?

The outcome was a locomotive with both the speed of the *Novelty* and the power to pull heavy loads. Passengers could now travel at speeds they had never dreamed of before.

Here are two responses, one from a young actress, Fanny Kemble, who was an admirer of Stephenson, the other from Thomas Greevey MP, one of the men responsible for the rejection of the original Liverpool and Manchester Railway Bill.

A *You cannot imagine how strange it seemed to be journeying on thus, without any visible cause of progress other than the magical machine with its flying white breath and rhythmical unvarying pace between these rocky walls [Olive Mount] . . . and when I reflected that these great masses of stone had been cut asunder to allow our passage thus far below the surface of the earth, I felt as if no fairy tale was half as wonderful as what I saw.*

The engine was set off at its utmost speed, 35 miles an hour, swifter than a bird flies. . . . You cannot conceive what the sensation of cutting the air was; the motion is as smooth

as possible too, I could either have read or written. When I closed my eyes the sensation of flying was quite delightful and strange beyond description. Yet strange as it was, I had a perfect sense of security and not the slightest fear.

B   Today we have had a 'lark' of a very high order. I had the satisfaction, for I can't call it a pleasure, of taking a trip of 5 miles . : . and we did it in just a quarter of an hour — that is twenty miles an hour . . . .

But the quickest motion is to me frightful; it is really like flying and it is impossible to divest yourself of the notion of instant death to all upon the least accident happening. It gave me a headache that has not left me yet. . . . The smoke is very inconsiderable indeed, but sparks of fire are abroad and in some quantity: one burnt Miss de Ros's cheek, another a hole in Lady Marian's silk pelisse. Altogether, I am extremely glad indeed to have seen this miracle and to have travelled in it . . . but having done so, I am quite satisfied with my first achievement being my last.

Quoted in F. Ferneyhough's book, *Liverpool and Manchester Railway 1830–1980*, 1980

1   Are there any points on which Miss Kemble and Mr Greevey agree?
2   What are the most significant points of disagreement?
3   Do you think that one of these accounts is likely to provide a more typical account of an early passenger's experience than the other one? Explain your answer.

The locomotive engine

The *Rocket* contained most of the features which were to be found in the successful locomotives of the next few years, although there were modifications and improvements. Consider Robert Stephenson's description of a locomotive made in 1838:

By causing all the flame and heated air to pass through a great number of tubes surrounded by water, a very great and rapid means of heating the water is obtained as a very large heated surface is thus exposed to the water.

Former locomotives with only a flue through the boiler have never been able to travel faster than about eight miles an hour as they had not sufficient heating surface in the boiler to generate the steam for supplying the cylinder more rapidly. . . . The introduction of tubes into the boiler is one of the greatest improvements that has been made in the construction of locomotives, and was the cause of the superiority of the *Rocket* engine to those that competed with it.

Impelling the piston

Having raised the steam it had to be made to drive the engine. Stephenson described this process as follows:

The piston is impelled by moving the slide valve from its central position, so as to admit steam ... into the cylinder through one of the ports ... and the steam pressing against the front of the piston impels it to the back end of the cylinder. The slide is then moved to the opposite position, covering over the front part and opening the back part in order to admit steam behind the piston and impel it back again to the fore end of the cylinder, at the same time allowing the steam in front of the piston, which is now waste steam, to escape by the inside of the slide and waste part O into the blast pipe, rushing out thence up the chimney.

Keeping a hot blast

The steam coming from the chimney can be used to create a draught and draw the fire through the tubes all the faster. Stephenson described the problem and how it was overcome:

The height of the chimney is obliged to be small, as it can never exceed fourteen feet height from the rails, so the draught produced is not all sufficient to urge the fire to the intense heat necessary to produce steam at the pressure and in the quantity required.

This is done by making the waste steam issue through the pipe, called the blast pipe, which is ... gradually contracted throughout its length to make the steam rush out with more force, causing a very powerful draught through the tubes and the fire.

Description of the Patent Locomotive Steam Engine
of Messrs. Robert Stephenson & Co., 1838

Using the evidence

Draw a simplified diagram of the locomotive to show the boiler and the route of the steam to the chimney. In an insert show the valve in both positions.

On the diagram, label the features which, according to Stephenson, made the locomotive much more efficient.

All this may seem simple to an engineer today. It certainly was not at the time. Indeed, the problem of fitting 25 tubes inside the boiler almost drove Robert Stephenson to despair:

[The tubes were] soldered to brass screws which were screwed into the boiler ends. When the tubes were thus fitted and the boiler filled with

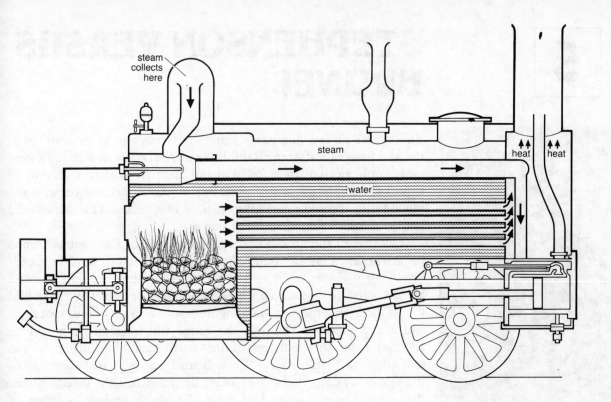

steam collects here

steam

heat   heat

water

Above: *A cross-section of Stephenson's engine. The routes of steam and smoke are indicated*

Right: *The valve in both positions*

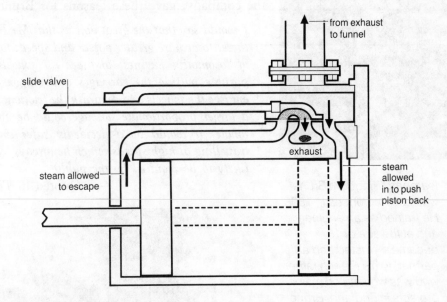

from exhaust to funnel

slide valve

exhaust

steam allowed to escape

steam allowed in to push piston back

water, hydraulic pressure was applied, but the water squirted out at every joint and the factory floor was flooded.

S. Smiles: *The Lives of George and Robert Stephenson*, 1857

Finally the problem was overcome by fitting tubes into holes bored in the boiler ends, and then soldering the joints — a good example of the trial and error methods used by early engineers.

5 STEPHENSON VERSUS BRUNEL

There were no revolutionary changes in the design of locomotives in the first few years after the Rainhill Trials. Certainly new engines were more sophisticated, more reliable and larger, but that is only to be expected with the passage of time. Furthermore, locomotives were not much faster. People were still suspicious of speed, and most trains did not go at much above 30 miles per hour.

It was when the great engineer Isambard Kingdom Brunel turned his attention to railway building that a new search for greater speeds began. Brunel was not a man to follow the example of others unless he saw good reason to, and he saw no good reason why he should follow the Stephensons in building lines with a gauge of four foot eight and a half inches. (This was the gauge which Stephenson said he adopted from the collieries of the north east. The origin of the measurement is uncertain.) When Brunel became Chief Engineer of the Great Western Railway in 1835, he persuaded the directors that they should have a seven foot gauge. Charles Saunders, secretary of the company, gave these reasons for Brunel's decision:

> *I would say that the great objects that Mr Brunel contemplated were these: to acquire greater power and speed; to improve the construction of locomotive engines; to place the wheels outside, or as near as possible outside the carriages and wagons in order that he might enlarge the wheels and diminish the friction; he expressed a belief that a larger proportionate stowage could be obtained; and that on the whole, it would be a decidedly safer and more secure mode of travelling at high speeds which he always looked forward to as being likely to be required by the public.*

Quoted in *The Spectator*, May 1846

Isambard Kingdom Brunel was born in Portsea in 1806. He trained as an engineer and at the age of 18 became a 'trusted and able partner' to his French father who was working on major projects in England. Brunel became one of the most versatile engineers of the 19th century, building railways, bridges, steamships and tunnels

Right: *One of Brunel's 7'0" gauge locomotives*

Brunel was little troubled by the prospect of confusion created by the two gauges. Indeed, he believed 'the spirit of emulation and competition ... will do more good to the public than the uniformity of system', and that 'the inconvenience and expense will be so trifling that it is hardly worth consideration'. Also, of course, he thought his competitors would finally change to a gauge of seven feet.

The moment of truth came in 1843 when the two gauges met at Bristol and Gloucester. The notorious 'change of gauge' became a national debating point. George Hudson, the 'Railway King' (see page 46), said:

> *I think the Public can scarcely overrate the inconvenience ... that is experienced from the transhipment of goods from Birmingham to Bristol. It crowds up the station and the unpacking of goods is most injurious.*

Part of the evidence put before the Royal Commission, 1845

Problems of the break of gauge

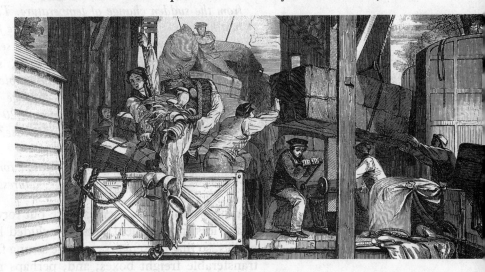

In June 1846 a reporter from the *Illustrated London News* witnessed the full inconvenience:

> *It is found at Gloucester that to tranship the contents of one wagon ... to the other, takes about an hour with all the force of porters you can put to work on it. An ordinary train of wagons [contains] bricks, slates, lime, chalk, or limestone and chalk, flags, clay, manure, salt, coal and coke, timber, dyewoods, iron ore, leads and metals, cast iron pots, grates and ovens, grindstones, brimstone, bones and hoofs, bark, hides and seal skins, oil cake, potatoes, onions and other vegetables, cheese, chairs, furniture, hardware, earthenware, dry salteries, groceries, provisions, cotton wool, wines, spirits, manufactured goods, fish, eggs, ripe fruit etc. etc.*
>
> *Now let us contemplate the loss by damage done to the goods on this one train alone by the break of gauge, causing the removal of every article. In the hurry the bricks are miscounted, the slates chipped*

at the edges, the cheeses cracked, the ripe fruit and vegetables crushed and spoiled, the chairs, furniture and oil cakes, cast iron pots, grates and ovens, all more or less broken, the coals turned into slack, the salt short of weight, sundry bottles of wine deficient, and the fish too late for market. The pigs object to Break of Gauge, and oxen resist terrifically, two hours having been spent in transhipping one of them.

As for passengers, an anonymous author wrote:

I would seek no more unbiased testimony against the break of gauge than what Mrs Brunel herself would furnish in making the journey at night with two of her children, servants and the usual amount of family luggage. I beseech her to take an evening train . . . and make the experiment. She arrives at Gloucester in darkness, the children are awakened to be properly muffled up in the transit from one carriage to the other; of course they are very fractious; they possibly catch cold from the sudden change of temperature. The servants are not in the best humour with their discomfort and are far less handy than usual. Every corner of the carriage has to be searched for bonnets, stray gloves, handkerchiefs, smelling bottles, sandwich cases, carriage basket, parasols, umbrellas and unutterable small parcels. With great difficulty and bustle the heavy luggage is huddled together and transferred. At last after a delay of some 20 minutes the party is on the road to Bristol. 'Where is the writing case?' In the hurry it has been left behind.

A Railway Traveller's Reason for Adopting Uniformity of Gauge, addressed to I. K. Brunel Esq.

Various astonishing schemes were put forward to make the break of gauge less inconvenient. These included having detachable carriage bodies, so that passengers could be swung from one chassis to another; transferable freight boxes; and, perhaps most dubious of all, telescopic axles.

In 1845 a Royal Commission was set up to hear evidence and make recommendations. It was during his own testimony that Brunel said: 'If experiments were made, it will be found that up to the present time, speed and economy and safety are attained to a much greater extent on the wide gauge than the narrow; and notwithstanding the opinions expressed, I believe that this can be proved by experiment under the eyes of the commission'.

The challenge having been made, the supporters of narrow gauge agreed to trials. The locomotive used for the broad gauge was the *Ixion*, which had been in use since 1840. On the narrow gauge a Stephenson 'Great A' was used. There is evidence to show that the narrow gauge trial was less than satisfactory. The engine did not make a standing start, and one of the observers, Daniel Gooch of the Great Western Railway, noted that at 47 miles per hour 'I find the engine exceedingly unsteady, so much so that I doubted the safety of it'.

The results of the trials were as follows:

York — Darlington, 44 miles, narrow gauge

Load	Average speed (m.p.h.)	Maximum speed
80 tons	43.25	50.75
50 tons	47	58

Paddington — Didcot, 53 miles, broad gauge

Load	Average speed (m.p.h.)	Maximum speed
81.5 tons	47.5	60
61 tons	52.4	67

Quoted in O.S. Nock's book, *Rocket 150*, 1980

The commission's final report came to the following conclusions:

1st   *That in regards the safety, accommodation and convenience of the passengers, no decided preference is due on either gauge; but that on the Broad Gauge the motion is generally more easy at high velocities.*

2nd   *That in respect of speed we consider the advantages are with the Broad Gauge; but we think that public safety would be endangered by employing the greater capabilities of the Broad Gauge much beyond their present use, except on roads more consolidated and more perfectly formed than those of the existing lines.*

3rd   *That, in the commercial case of the transport of goods, we believe the Narrow Gauge to possess the greater convenience, and to be the more suited to the general traffic of the country.*

Report of the Commission in favour
of National Uniformity of Railway Gauge, 2 May 1846

Brunel was defeated, and by 1892 the seven foot gauge had disappeared, to the sorrow of many admirers. However, Brunel's Great Western Railway, with its magnificent bridges, tunnels and stations, is still with us to remind us of the vision of the most versatile engineer of the age.

Questions

1   In the paragraph above Brunel is described as a man of great vision, in contrast to the much more down-to-earth Stephenson. Is there any evidence in the sources quoted in this chapter to support this view?

2 Many people were dismayed by the 'break of gauge'. Using the evidence in this chapter and your own ideas, write an argument against the break of gauge and for a uniform system.

3 Look at the table below, the appendix to the Royal Commission's report.

a) In what way does the appendix support the conclusions?

b) Does it provide any other reasons for the verdict apart from those stated in the report?

APPENDIX TO THE REPORT

RETURN OF RAILWAYS IN GREAT BRITAIN, FURNISHED BY THE
BOARD OF TRADE, JULY 1845.

Grand total of Railways made, sanctioned, or likely to be sanctioned, up to present time, July 1845.

On the narrow gauge of 4 foot 8½ inches	4,131¼
On the wide gauge of 7 foot	777

STATEMENT OF ACCIDENTS.

Abstracted from the Reports of the Railway Department of the Board of Trade, in which the Engine and Carriages or some part of the Train have run off the line, without any known obstruction, from September 1840 to March 1845.

Date of Accident.		Name of Railway.	Breadth of Gauge.	Deaths and Injuries.		Nature and Cause of the Accident.
				Killed.	Injured.	
19 Oct.	1840	Eastern Counties	5 ft. 0 in.	1	6	Excessive Speed.
8 Nov.	1840	Midland Counties	4 ft. 8½ in.	–	8	Excessive Speed.
7 Sept.	1841	Great Western	7 ft. 0 in.	1	–	One engine out of two off the line.
2 Oct.	1841	London and Brighton	4 ft. 8½ in.	1	2	Bad road and excessive speed.
15 Nov.	1843	South-eastern.	4 ft. 4½ in.	–	–	Cause not known.
31 Oct.	1844	Newcastle and Carlisle	4 ft. 8½ in.	–	1	Excessive speed.

Similar Accidents which have occurred since the last Report of the Board of Trade, from March 1845 to 1st January 1846.

16 June	1845	Great Western	7 ft. 0 in.	–	several	Express train carriages only off the line.
June	1845	Great Western	7 ft. 0 in.	–	–	Ditto, a similar accident, not reported.
4 Aug.	1845	Northern and East	4 ft. 8½ in.	8	several	Cause not ascertained.
10 Aug.	1845	Northern and Eastern	4 ft. 8½ in.	–	2	Supposed cause, a defective joint. Less speed recommended.
18 Aug.	1845	Manchester and Leeds	4 ft. 8½ in.	–	several	Express trains, thrown over an embankment.
Dec.	1845	Norfolk	4 ft. 8½ in.			Experimental train, speed 48 miles.
1 Jan.	1846	York and Darlington	4 ft. 8½ in.	2	3	

SPEED OF EXPRESS TRAINS.

Table showing the Speed of Express Trains on the following Lines, as deduced from their respective Time-tables.

Name of Railway.		Station.	Distance. Miles	Time. h.	Time. m.	Rate per hour. Miles.	
GREAT WESTERN.			*Broad Gauge.*				
Paddington		to Didcot	53	1	7	47.5	No stoppage.
Didcot	...	to Swindon	24	0	35	41.1	One stoppage.
Swindon	...	to Bath	29.75	0	37	48.2	No stoppage.
Bath	..	to Bristol	11.6	0	20	34.5	One stoppage.
Bristol	..	to Taunton	44.76	0	58	46.3	No stoppage.
Taunton		to Exeter	30.75	0	47	39.2	One stoppage.
LONDON & BIRMINGHAM.			*Narrow Gauge.*				
London	..	to Tring	31½	0	48	39.6	
Tring	..	to Wolverton	20½	0	40	30.75	One stoppage.
Wolverton	..	to Coventry	41½	0	57	43.7	One stoppage.
Coventry	..	to Birmingham	18½	0	35	34.4	One stoppage.

	Great Western.		London and Birmingham.
Ratio of cost of engine and carriage plant	1	to	.763
Do. of repairs of do. for two years	1	to	1.011
Do. of cost of locomotive power for do.	1	to	.940
Do. of passengers mileage for do.	1	to	.945
Do. of total passengers revenues for do.	1	to	1.072

6

EFFECTS OF THE RAILWAY REVOLUTION

The speed with which the railway network was established was truly remarkable. So too were the effects of this new system of communication. Everybody was affected in some way or other by the railways — as a traveller, as a manufacturer or purchaser of goods, as an observer of the landscape, as a writer of letters, or as part of a society that was industrialising rapidly.

The traveller

According to one estimate, the national total of coach passengers in 1833 was 2 688 000. To this should be added a further 25 or 30 per cent of travellers using post horses, canal boats and other forms of transport, giving a total of three and a quarter million travellers. Thirty years later the number of travellers on the railways alone was 204 635 075.

The number of passengers took the railway companies by surprise, and at first there was a shortage of locomotives and rolling stock to cope with the demand. Possibly the main reason for the large number of passengers was the novelty of railway travel. On the Liverpool and Manchester Railway some trains were put on simply to run down the line to the most spectacular sights, such as the Sankey Viaduct. Scheduled services were packed, and extra trains were put on for all sorts of different reasons — for example, to take people to the races; to carry an opera company; to take people to see the steamship Great

The Crimple Valley Viaduct

THE RAILWAY MONITOR.

To Travellers.

THE existing railway arrangements render it imperative that you should provide yourselves with a large stock of philosophy, to enable you to put up with certain inconveniences, which you will be sure, to a greater or less extent, to encounter on most lines, and whereof a classification is hereby appended for your benefit.

FIRST CLASS.

THE chief inconvenience peculiar to this class, is, that your fare will be about twice as much as you ought in fairness to pay. You run, perhaps, rather less risk in this class than in the others, of having your neck broken; but you must not be unprepared for such a contingency.

SECOND CLASS.

IN travelling by the second class, you will do well to wear a respirator, unless you wish to be choked with dust and ashes from the engine close in front of you. Also, if you are going far, you are recommended to put on a diving-dress, like that used at the Polytechnic; because, if it should rain much during your journey, the sides of the carriage being open, you will have to ride in a pool of water. Your dignity must not be hurt, should you have for next neighbour a ragamuffin in handcuffs, with a policeman next him. The hardness of your seat is a mere trifle; that is the least of the annoyances to which you are judiciously subjected, with the view of driving you into the first class train.

THIRD CLASS.

Make up your mind for unmitigated hail, rain, sleet, snow, thunder and lightning. Look out for a double allowance of smoke, dust, dirt, and everything that is disagreeable. Be content to run a twofold risk of loss of life and limb. Do not expect the luxury of a seat. As an individual and a traveller, you are one of the lower classes; a poor, beggarly, contemptible person, and your comfort and convenience are not to be attended to.

ALL THREE CLASSES.

Punctuality may be the soul of business, but suppose not that it is the spirit of railways. If you do not care whether you keep an appointment or not, make it on the faith of the Company, by all means; but otherwise by none. Regard starting, or arriving at your destination, only half an hour too late, as luck. You pay nothing extra to attendants for civility, so you must not hope for it. Remember that you are at the mercy of the Company as to where you may stop for refreshments; for which, accordingly, be not surprised if you have to pay through the nose. Beware, if you quit the train for an instant, lest it move on; you have paid your money, the rest is your own look-out, and, you may depend will be no one else's. For loss and damage of luggage, and the like little mishaps, prepare yourself as a matter of course; and if at the end of your journey you find yourself in a whole skin—thank your stars.

Railway classes according to Punch

Britain (built by Brunel) in port at Liverpool; to take people to the assizes or to an election.

Whether for business or pleasure, so many passengers paid to travel by rail that the company was able to announce substantial profits. This in turn encouraged the railway builders.

In the early days of the railway, there were only two classes of train on the Liverpool and Manchester line.

Fares

First Class Train, Coaches, Four inside	6s. 6d.
First Class Train, Coaches, Six inside	5s. 6d.
Second Class Train, Glass Coaches	5s. 6d.
Second Class Train, Open Coaches	4s. 0d.
Charge for conveyance of 4-wheeled carriages	20s. 0d.
Charge for conveyance of 2-wheeled carriages	15s. 0d.

These prices were too high for poorer people and it was not until about 1844 that the government stepped in to provide for them. This was the year the 'Railway Plunder Bill', as its enemies called it, was passed. The bill made provision of third class travel compulsory, and fixed a minimum speed and maximum price of a penny a mile, as well as enforcing safety regulations. Despite the uncomfortable conditions of third class railway wagons, the response was great and the number of passengers increased still further.

The document on page 37 relating to the break of gauge gives some idea of the variety of goods carried by the railway. Even so, this aspect of railway work was not, as anticipated by the railway companies, the main source of income. Passenger travel was more profitable. This was due partly to competition from the canals, where prices were cut to the extent that railways had only the advantage of speed, which was not required in the transportation of some goods.

The class system at work, according to the Illustrated London News

1st class

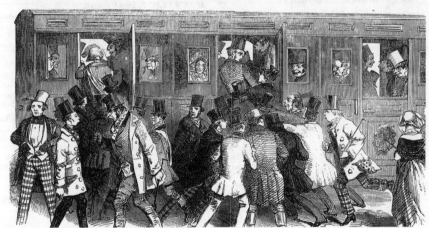

2nd class

3rd class

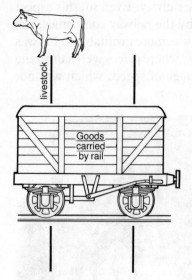

livestock

Goods carried by rail

Questions
Look at the cartoons on pages 42 and 43.
1. In *The Railway Monitor*, what is the overall attitude of the writer towards railways? Give brief quotations to support your answer.
2. Is there any factual material in this document?
3. Does the cartoon from the *Illustrated London News* provide any further information about the conditions of travel? What seems to be the standpoint of this cartoonist?
4. Look back at the document on page 37 concerning the break of gauge. Use the information it contains to draw a pattern-diagram showing the types of goods carried on the railway. The one in the margin has already been started.
5. Use a textbook of nineteenth century history to identify the meaning of the term *laissez-faire*. What is the significance of the Railway Act of 1844 in this context?

The class system, as demonstrated by the London and Southampton Railway's timetable

ON AND AFTER THE 12TH OF OCTOBER,

The Hours of Departure will be as follows: —

DOWN TRAINS, from Vauxhall.			UP TRAINS, to Vauxhall.		
To Southampton (*Mixed Train*)	8	Morn.	From Southampton (*Mail*)	2	Morn.
To Woking Common (*do.*)	9 30	"	From Southampton (*Mixed Train*)	6	"
To Southampton (*First Class Train*)	11	"	From Woking Common (*do.*)	7 45	"
To Southampton (*Goods*)	12	"	From Southampton (*Goods*)	10	"
To Southampton (*Mixed Train*)	1	After.	From Southampton (*First Class*)	11	"
To Southampton (*First Class*)	3	"	From Woking Common (*Mixed Train*)	12	"
To Woking Common (*Mixed Train*)	4	"	From Southampton (*do.*)	1 30	After.
To Southampton (*do.*)	5	"	From Southampton (*First Class*)	3	"
To Southampton (*Mail*)	8 30	"	From Southampton (*Mixed Train*)	6	"
To Southampton (*Goods*)	8 45	"	From Southampton (*Goods*)	8	"

The *First Class Trains* will perform the journey in three hours, taking *First Class Passengers* only, excepting that accommodation will be afforded for a limited number of Servants in Livery, 13s. each. These Trains will not call at any Stations between London and Woking Common, but will take up and set down Passengers at all the Stations between Woking Common and Southampton.

The *Mixed Trains* will call at all the Stations, except the Train which leaves London at 8 o'clock, a.m., which will stop at any Station, in case Passengers are waiting to go to the west of Woking Common.

Third Class Passengers will be taken by the Goods' Trains.

SUNDAY TRAINS.

DOWN.			UP.		
To Southampton (*Mixed Train*)	10	Morn.	From Southampton (*Mail*)	2	Morn.
To Woking Common (*do.*)	10 30	"	From Woking Common (*Mixed Train*)	9	"
To Southampton (*Goods*)	12	"	From Southampton (*do.*)	10	"
To Southampton (*Mixed Train*)	5	After.	From Southampton (*Goods*)	10	"
To Woking Common (*do.*)	7 30	"	From Southampton (*Mixed Train*)	5	After.
To Southampton (*Mail*)	8 30	"	From Woking Common (*do.*)	6	"
To Southampton (*Goods*)	8 45	"	From Southampton (*Goods*)	8	"

FARES.

		FAST TRAIN	MIXED TRAIN		GOODS TR.
Distance.	STATIONS.	1st Class.	1st Class.	2nd Class.	3rd Class.
		s. d.	s. d.	s. d.	s. d.
Miles.					
3	London to Wandsworth	...	1 0	0 6	...
6	...... Wimbledon	...	1 6	1 0	...
10	...... Kingston	...	2 0	1 6	...
13	...... Esher and Hampton Court	...	2 6	1 6	...
15½	...... Walton	...	3 0	2 0	...
17½	...... Weybridge	...	3 6	2 0	...
23	...... Woking	6 0	5 0	3 6	2 6
31½	...... Farnborough	8 6	7 6	5 0	3 0
38	...... Winchfield	10 0	9 0	6 0	3 6
46	...... Basingstoke	12 0	11 0	7 0	4 0
56	...... Andover Road	15 0	13 6	9 0	5 0
64	...... Winchester	17 6	15 6	10 0	6 0
76¾	...... Southampton	20 0	18 0	12 0	7 0

Railways and the economy

It is generally accepted that their impact was greater than that of any other single innovation of the period.

T.R. Gourvich: *Railways and the British Economy*, 1980

The transport of passengers and goods by railway literally speeded up the economy. What had taken days now took only hours, and people such as businessmen and factory owners found the pace of investment, demand and supply increasing, to their great satisfaction and profit.

The railways also generated high employment. A House of Commons return gave the numbers employed on lines under construction in 1847 as 256 509, or about four per cent of the working male population.

This figure of course deals only with those directly employed, and omits the workers involved in running the railways, and those in the industries which fed the railways: iron and steel; coal; timber; engineering; glass; building, and so on. Between 1844 and 1851 over one quarter of pig-iron produced in Britain was for the railways. Skilled as well as unskilled workers were in great demand. Railways needed engineers, surveyors, lawyers, accountants and a host of other highly trained people.

One of the most significant long-term effects of railways on the economy was in the field of capital formation.

capital formation: when money is invested in equipment, which will in its turn make a profit for investors; for example, buying factories and machinery to produce goods

Railway investment in the second half of the [1840s] leapt ahead to great dominance, taking at its height in 1847 not far short of 7% of national income ....

B.R. Mitchell: *The Coming of the Railway and U.K. Economic Growth*, 1964

At one time the desire to invest in and profit from railways reached ridiculous heights; this was known as 'railway mania'.

vortex whirlpool

A reckless spirit of gambling set in, which completely changed the character and objects of railway enterprise. The public outside the Stock Exchange also became infected and many persons utterly ignorant of railways, knowing and caring nothing about their national uses, but hungering and thirsting after premiums, rushed into the vortex. They applied for allotments, and subscribed for shares in lines, of the engineering character and probable traffic of which they knew nothing. Provided they could but obtain allotments which they could sell at a premium and put the profit into their pocket, it was enough for them .... The mania affected all ranks. It embraced merchants and manufacturers, gentry and shopkeepers, clerks in public office and loungers at clubs.

Folly and knavery were, for a time, completely in the ascendant. The sharpers of society were let loose .... They threw out railway schemes as lures to catch the unwary. They fed the mania with a

George Hudson: the 'Railway King' at one time controlled one-fifth of Britain's railways. However, he misused invested money, paying shareholders instead of investing in capital equipment and railway lines. When investors found out and lost confidence in him, his empire collapsed

constant succession of new projects. . . . Then was the harvest time of scheming lawyers, parliamentary agents, engineers, surveyors and traffic-takers who were ready to take up any railway scheme, however desperate, and to prove any amount of traffic where none existed.
S. Smiles: *The Lives of George and Robert Stephenson*, 1857

Many people lost their savings. However, more careful investors could still make a profit, especially by investing in overseas projects. Britain was soon to become railway builder to the world and the effect which this had on employment was remarkable.

'Railway Mania', according to Punch

Questions

1 Summarise the indirect effects of railways on the economy.
2 Why were the railways so significant in the field of capital formation, and why, in this connection, did the 'Railway King' lose his crown?
3 According to Smiles, who is to blame for railway mania?
4 What is the *Punch* cartoonist trying to say about railway mania?

Effects of railways on towns and cities

A few towns, such as Lincoln, resisted the arrival of railways and remained, for a few years, fairly unaltered. For other towns the change brought about by railways was considerable. At the centre of these towns the railway terminus became a new point of focus, and the use of land and property nearby changed.

Attracted to the termini were retail shopkeepers and transit warehouses; repelled were residential and, on the whole, business users.
J.R. Kellett: *The Impact of Railways on Victorian Cities*, 1969

Other forms of traffic — cabs, carts and horse omnibuses — now found a new source of employment at the termini:

The increased flood of immigrant passengers from the provinces and the torrent of goods that kept pouring in to the great emporium of the capital . . . caused an utterly new phase of traffic.
J.R. Kellett: *The Impact of Railways 'on Victorian Cities*, 1969

In the approaches to the termini the appearance of many towns and cities were altered. In some places buildings were compulsorily purchased to be knocked down and replaced by railway lines. Elsewhere other new features appeared:

. . . a massive new feature of the urban scene [was] the railway viaduct, striding past working class houses at roof top level. Occasionally these great stone viaducts were constructed to ensure the right elevation for crossing a river or for entering a terminal site, but usually

Congestion near the terminus

The city viaduct

their main purpose was to avoid street closures. But the effects on the area it crossed were dilapidating in the extreme.
J.R. Kellett: *The Impact of Railways on Victorian Cities*, 1969

As the following extract shows, the railways did bring some movement out of the main towns to existing centres of population. However, the railway suburbs did not really begin to grow until the 1860s.

In Manchester, where the middle classes did begin to move outwards, they relied on horse omnibuses which went to Pendleton, Rusholme, etc. Apart from the Altrincham branch of the Manchester South Junction, opened in the late 1840s, there was little attempt to develop dormitory traffic.
J.R. Kellett: *The Impact of Railways on Victorian Cities*, 1969

Indeed, in London the railway companies refused to run third class trains to certain suburbs because of the effect it would have. In evidence given by the General Manager of the Great Eastern Railway Company, who was refusing to put on a working man's train to Noel Park, he justified his decision by saying:

I imagine that no one living in Noel Park could desire to possess the same class of neighbours as the residents of Stamford Hill. The reports current in the district of the men residing there are of a character that would deter anyone wishing for neighbours of that kind in any part.
Royal Commission on Working Class Housing, 1884

When asked if existing residents of Noel Park would prefer to pay more rather than have third class passengers living near them, the General Manager replied: 'I should think so, and hope so.'

There were some towns which grew up almost entirely because of the railways. Crewe, for example, developed because it was a railway

47

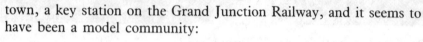

Crewe station

town, a key station on the Grand Junction Railway, and it seems to have been a model community:

> The number of workmen employed is 1600. About a hundred yards [from the workshops] there stands a plain, neat building erected by the company, containing baths, hot, cold and shower, for the workmen as well as their wives and daughters. To a medical man was given a house and surgery, in addition to which he receives from every unmarried workman 1d per week, if married with a family, 2d a week, for which he undertakes to give attendance and medicine to whatever may require them.
>
> A clergyman with an adequate salary from the company super-intends three large day schools. There is also a library and mechanics institute [and] a vocal and instrumental class.
>
> The town of Crewe contains 514 houses, one church, three schools and one Town Hall, all belonging to the Company.
>
> F.B. Head: *Stokers and Pokers*, 1849

Railways also had an important effect on the architecture of cities, towns and villages, and of course on the landscape as a whole. Here are two memorable examples.

Above: *The Abbotcliffe Tunnel*

Right: *Building the Menai Bridge*

Questions

1 Copy this diagram and label the type of changes brought about by the railways.

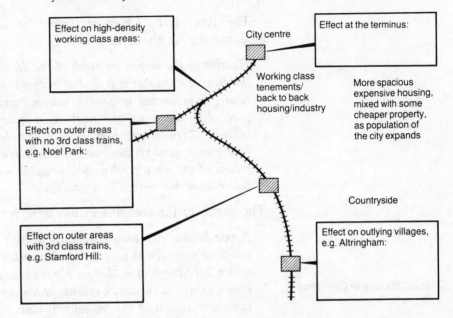

Effect on high-density working class areas:

City centre

Effect at the terminus:

Working class tenements/ back to back housing/industry

More spacious expensive housing, mixed with some cheaper property, as population of the city expands

Effect on outer areas with no 3rd class trains, e.g. Noel Park:

Countryside

Effect on outer areas with 3rd class trains, e.g. Stamford Hill:

Effect on outlying villages, e.g. Altringham:

2 What do the evidence of the General Manager of the Great Eastern Railway on page 47 and the schedule for the London and Southampton Railway on page 44 show about the railway directors' attitude to the lower classes?

3 Using your knowledge of conditions in the cities of the 1840s, describe the advantages of living at Crewe.

4 Consult a local history book or use your own observation to assess the impact of the railway where you live. Consider these questions: when did the railway arrive? Did it cause the area to grow? Was there a change in the use of land? How did it affect the appearance of your locality?

Improved communication

penny post: before 1840 the cost of postage was very high. Then a standard rate of one penny was introduced for all letters. The postage was paid by the sender who bought a stamp. The system could not have worked efficiently without the railways

As well as the obvious advantages of travel, the railways made written communication much easier. The Liverpool and Manchester Railway first carried post in 1830, and the volume increased greatly with the introduction of stamps and the 'penny post' in 1840. Newspapers were first carried in 1831, and it was not long before the *Railway Times* was published.

Signalling created the need for a new system of communication down the line, and the electric telegraph met this need. An unusual example of its effectiveness can be seen in this strange case.

A murder was committed in Slough. However, the murderer botched his job, and his victim screamed before falling down dead. Neighbours heard the scream and saw the man leaving the house for the station.

The Rev. E.T. Champier, vicar of Upton-cum-Chorley, gave evidence during the trial:

Hearing of the suspicious death of the deceased and that a person in the dress of a Quaker was the last man who had been seen to leave the house, I proceeded to Slough station, thinking it likely he might proceed to town by the railway. I saw him pass through the office.... He left for London in a first class carriage. Mr Howell [the station master] then sent off a full description of this person by means of the electric telegraph, to cause him to be watched by the police upon his arrival at Paddington.

The words of the communication were precisely as follows:

A murder has just been committed at Salt Hill, and the suspected murderer was seen to take a first class ticket for London by the train which left Slough at 7.42 p.m. He is in the garb of a Quaker with a brown greatcoat on, which reaches nearly down to his feet; he is in the last compartment of the second first class carriage.

The arrival of the Christmas train

The reply:

The up-train has arrived; and a person answering the description came out of the compartment mentioned. I pointed the man out to Sergeant Williams. The man got into a New Road omnibus and Sergeant Williams into the same.

As for the murderer ...

Everybody who has travelled on the Great Western Railway knows how joyously its trains skim along the level country between Slough and London. He no doubt appreciated the speed more than any of his fellow passengers. He probably felt that no power on earth could overtake him.

F.B. Head: *Stokers and Pokers*, 1849

Imagine his surprise on reaching home to see a policeman who confronted him with the words: 'Haven't you just come from Slough?' He was arrested, tried, found guilty and hanged. He had been overtaken by technology.

Question
What was made possible by the increased ability to communicate? Use examples from this chapter, and add some suggestions of your own.

Fears and hopes: the first years of railways

Did the predictions of those who opposed the railways come true? The opposition had forecast danger and death. They were proved correct on one of the most important days in railway history, the day of the opening of the Liverpool and Manchester Railway.

Lord Palmerston described the incident in which the MP William Huskisson was killed:

Huskisson: MP for Liverpool and President of the Board of Trade. He was highly respected and played an important part in improving the rules of foreign trading

As I was present with him from the moment he entered the car till that of the accident, of which I was an immediate eye witness, you will perhaps feel a melancholy interest in having some of the details.

We were at a place where the railroad goes through a quarry ... about 50 persons were walking about while the engine took in water, when it was observed that another engine was coming along at speed on the parallel line. Everybody entered as soon as they could, or stood still between the cars.... I pulled in Esterhazy, who was after me. I then saw Huskisson seize the wicket, which was about four feet long, and in great trepidation try to get round it into the car, instead of standing still as he ought. It was too late — the engine had

wicket: carriage door

51

come up and either knocked him down or he fell on its road in front, on his back, in trying to cross its line out of its way. His left leg and thigh ... lay across the rail — the whole passed over him — he was then seen with his leg and thigh reduced to pulp ... a more horrible spectacle was never witnessed ... the papers tell the rest correctly. He was carried to Eccles, a place within four miles of Manchester by the Railroad, at a speed of 35 miles an hour ... He died a quarter before 9, having survived the accident exactly nine hours.

Quoted in R.H.G. Thomas's book, *The Liverpool and Manchester Railway*, 1980

Other accidents occurred in these early years for a variety of reasons: faulty components, poor signalling, human error, fog, brake failure. Several fatalities occurred because of the stupidity of passengers or people walking along the lines, including a man doing a tightrope walk along the line in Olive Mount. In spite of all this, in a typical year such as 1840, *The Manchester Guardian* was able to report:

1,052,000 passengers were conveyed upon the Liverpool — Manchester Railway with but one accident, and that was the case of a passenger who jumped out of a second class train, whilst at full speed, to save himself a few miles' walk.

The arrival of the working men's train

52

It cannot be denied that serious accidents did occur.

On June 10, 1845, the luggage van of an express train, with a great number of passengers, [going at] nearly 70 miles an hour, ran off the rail.... It ran for half a mile unperceived on the timbers without displacing the carriages till it came into contact with a girder at a bridge, when the wheel ran into the ballast: fortunately the engine and tender separated from the carriages, but so sudden and fearful was the catastrophe that the two first class [carriages] and one second class carriage were thrown with fearful violence off the line and down an embankment about fifteen feet in depth with an alarming crash. One of the carriages turned twice over and remained with its wheel in the air; one of the carriages was thrown completely across the line of rail. No lives were lost, but forty persons were more or less injured.

R. Ritchie: *Railways, Their Rise, Progress and Construction,* 1846

Enquiries were held into any such accidents. Failures in equipment brought rapid improvement, such as better rails or signalling. Human error was punished; drivers who went too fast were sacked; negligence on the part of any railway staff met with fines or dismissal. One driver, who was found guilty of manslaughter when he ran down passengers standing on the line, was imprisoned, until on appeal he was found not guilty and acquitted.

Considering the forces at work, it is remarkable that there were not more frequent accidents. As it was, the newspapers and cartoonists made much of them and a fear of speed remained in the minds of a few, as shown in this anonymous poem written in 1846:

John: *Blest be those times, Dick, when at early morn,*
       Rang through the silent streets the mailguard's horn,
       And passengers aroused just heard the strain,
       Settled their nightcaps and straight snored again.
       No demon whistle then their slumber broke,
       Its trembling victims no concussion woke,
       No smoking carriages bestrewed the ground,
       No mangled limbs were lost and never found.

Dick: *How gaily would our beauties bound along,*
       Obedient to the postboy's spur and thong;
       Or if perchance a screw on turnpike fell,
       They pulled him up again and all was well;
       Whilst on the railroad, if a screw get loose,
       You've every chance of running to the deuce.

John: *Yes, that's a fact, the papers day by day*
       Tell us how railroad screws have given way.
       Now bursts a boiler, o'er the embankment's ridge
       Rushes the hapless train, now falls a bridge;
       Now sinks a viaduct; or wrapt in fire,
       Or plunged in torrents, passengers expire.

Dick: *Ye who're not weary of dear life, forswear*
The locomotive, and ye lovely fair,
Who teeth and noses would preserve, to you
This counsel I address — the train eschew.
Old, young or neither, fat, thin, short, or tall,
Travel by turnpike, or not at all;
Or if you must by railway travel, still
Think what may happen and — first make your will.

The decline of the great age of coaching, so regretted by John and Dick, had been one of the chief fears of the opposition. Samuel Smiles, in his biography of the Stephensons, dismissed these and most of the other fears as being totally unfounded:

The proprietors of the canals were astounded by the fact that, notwithstanding the immense traffic conveyed by rail, their own traffic and receipts continued to increase.... The cattle owners were equally amazed to find the price of horse-flesh increasing with the extension of railways, and that the number of coaches running to and from the new railway stations gave employment to a greater number of horses than under the old stage-coach system. Those who prophesied the decay of the metropolis and the ruin of suburban cabbage growers ... were also disappointed; for while the new roads let citizens out of London, they let country people in. If the dear, suburban-grown cabbages became depreciated in value, there were truck loads of fresh grown country cabbages [coming to the city]. The food of the metropolis became rapidly improved, especially in the supply of wholesome meat and vegetables.

The prophecies of ruin and disaster to landlords and families were equally confounded by the openings of railways ... the farmers were enabled to buy their coals, lime and manure for less money, while they obtained a readier access to the best markets. Cows gave milk as before, their sheep fed and fattened, and even skittish horses ceased to shy at the passing locomotive.

Landlords also found that they could get higher rents for farms situated near a railway.... Land was now advertised for sale with the attraction of being 'near a railway station'.... Even Colonel Sibthorpe [the MP for Lincoln, and one of the staunchest opponents of the railways] was eventually compelled to acknowledge its utility. For a time he continued to post to and from the country as before. Then he compromised ... by taking a railway ticket for the long journey, and posting only a stage or two nearest town; until at length he undisguisedly committed himself ... to the express train, and performed the journey throughout upon what he had formerly de-nounced as 'the infernal railroad'.

S. Smiles: *The Lives of George and Robert Stephenson,* 1857

Shrewsbury railway station

Questions

1 Why do you think that accidents such as those described in this book had little effect on passenger demand for railways? Explain your answer carefully, using evidence from each case. You may wish to use modern parallels.

2 What makes the poem on pages 53 and 54 such effective anti-railway propaganda?

3 Take a double page in your exercise book. Use the whole of this chapter to construct a pattern-diagram showing the effects of the railways. This could become a useful plan for an essay on the subject.

INDEX

Numbers in **bold** denote illustrations